101 Quick & Easy

Cupcake and Muffin Recipes

Victoria Steele

COOKBOOK series

VICTORIA STEELE

CONTENTS

FROSTING & FILLINGS

MUFFINS

Quick & Easy Cupcakes and Muffins

Cupcakes are just the thing to add a festive touch to your next party. Simple or elaborate, they're colorful and tasty desserts that are just the right size to take in hand for casual entertaining.

Whether you decorate them with a quick layer of frosting or adorn each with custom flowers and artistic touches, your cupcake desserts will be the hit of your next get together.

Create a garden of blossoms or sculpt frosting animals and cartoon characters. You're only limited by your imagination. If you're new to cake decorating, cupcakes give you ample opportunities to practice, and, best of all, you can eat your mistakes and leave no evidence.

If cupcakes are a bit rich for your taste, fill your dessert craving with a muffin. You'll find loads of tasty muffin recipes from healthful bran and whole grain to delicious fruit and berry versions. And, of course there are specialty recipes like peanut butter and coffeecake, and of course, chocolate.

When it comes to frosting, you'll find flavors that will please everyone. Chocolate, buttercream and mocha are just a few of the recipes. There's also specialty frostings like pineapple and peanut butter to give your cupcakes a special flair. So, choose a recipe, get out your baking supplies and start creating little bites of decadent dessert deliciousness. Make sure to double the recipe, as they're sure to disappear almost as quickly as you finish them.

Frosting

Cupcakes are a delight right out of the paper holder – warm and rich; a good recipe doesn't even need any frosting. Well, maybe you need just a little frosting to turn up the sweet factor. Oh, who's kidding whom – you can never be too rich, too thin or have too much frosting.

Different frosting recipes have different textures and behave according to their density and dryness. Some softer frosting recipes, such as cream cheese frosting, don't have the density to stand up to piled-high peaks of sugary goodness. Decorator's buttercream frosting, on the other hand is perfect for piling on to create sculptural sweeties.

We've compiled a great selection of frosting recipes with all sorts of flavors and ingredients. Some recipes are simply meant for spreading on top of your cupcake for quick and delicious snacking, while other recipes can be flavored, tinted and used to make artistic confections for a special celebration.

Use the right frosting recipe for decorating your cupcakes. Pay attention to instructions and guides for beginners. Soon, you'll be piping flowers, designs and creating custom characters with ease.

Frosting Tools

Once you've decided on which frosting recipe to use, you'll need to assemble your frosting tools. These supplies are readily available at craft stores and baking supply shops. There are tons of tips and accessories available, but you only need a few tips and other supplies to get started.

Frosting Bags

If you're planning to do a lot of decorating, you may want to invest in heavy decorating bags. These are washable and reusable. If you're just in it for the short haul or doing small batches, you can purchase disposable piping bags. These can also be washed and reused, but they're not nearly as durable as the heavy decorating bags.

Couplers

Couplers are handy to have on hand if you tend to change out your tips. These little fittings slip in the pastry bag before you add your frosting. The end of the coupler protrudes out of the bag, which makes it easy for you to change piping tips mid-squeeze.

Frosting Tips

Here's where you can go a little crazy. There are about a half zillion tip sizes and shapes available, and you may be tempted to try each and every one. The good news is that they're not too costly. The better news is that you really only need a few tips and a little practice to create a huge variety of piping shapes and designs.

Start out with a small selection from small to jumbo, and practice varying your pressure and angle to create as many shapes and designs as you can. As you get comfortable, you'll find that you don't need to change your tips so much and can do a great deal with just a couple of tip varieties.

Let's Get Started

If you don't plan to change tips, you don't need to use a coupler. Just pop your tip in the pastry bag and set it in the opening. (A good tip to use is a large Wilton 1M star decorating tip.) Fold back the edge of your bag into a cuff three or four inches wide. Pop the bag into an empty glass with the cuff hanging over the edge. Now you can fill your bag easily with no mess. Only fill it about half full. You need plenty of material to twist or fold to keep your frosting pressure constant.

When you have your bag filled and sealed shut, you need to ensure there are no air bubbles trapped inside the bag. Squeeze out a bit of frosting back into the frosting bowl and you're ready to start.

If you keep a moist paper towel draped over your frosting bowl, you won't need to worry about your frosting drying out and crusting over.

A good way to practice the art of decorative frosting is to use parchment paper. You can squirt to your heart's content, and when you're finished, simply scrape the frosting back into the bowl and you're ready for round two.

If you make a mistake on a cupcake, rather than disposing of the evidence in your mouth, you can simply turn the cupcake upside down and drop the frosting back into the frosting bowl. When you start over, any little trace of the first attempt will be covered up with your new, improved creation.

A Word about Beating and Creaming

Both the words beating and creaming can be a little confusing if you aren't a chef or don't cook a lot. Here is a quick tutorial on both.

Beating – Unless a recipe says "beat at a medium speed" or "beat by hand", you can beat with an electric mixer or by hand. If the batter is thick, you probably want to beat it by hand with a wooden spoon or fork. If it is thin, you can use a mixer.

Creaming – Creaming is one of the most important steps in the entire recipe. Many cupcake and muffin recipes say "cream butter and sugar until fluffy and light." As with beating, creaming can be done with an electric mixer or by hand. If you are creaming by hand, slice the butter and let the butter or margarine reach room temperature (but not too warm). Beat the butter until it is soft. Then add the sugar and beat the mixture until it is fluffy and light and volume has increased. Be sure to scrape the bowl periodically.

To cream with a mixer, use cold butter or margarine. Mix on low or medium-low just until butter is softened, about 1 minute. Increase mixer to medium and add the sugar gradually to the butter and beat for 1 to 2 minutes until fluffy and lighter in color.

The best creaming method for beginners is to cream with a mixer using cold butter. If the room temperature butter is too warm, it may not cream well.

CUPCAKES

Chocolate Cupcakes

Brownie Cupcakes

These cupcakes are loaded with chopped pecans and are the best brownie cupcakes even without frosting.

Suggested frosting: Mocha Buttercream Frosting

1 3/4 cups sugar
1 cup flour
4 eggs
4 (1 oz.) squares semisweet chocolate
1 cup butter
1 cup chopped pecans
1 teaspoon vanilla

Combine sugar, flour and eggs. In a saucepan, melt chocolate and butter; add nuts. Combine the dry mixture and chocolate mixture; add vanilla. Fill muffin cups lined with paper cupcake liners two-thirds full of batter. Bake in preheated oven at 325 degrees F for 25 to 30 minutes.

Yield: 24 cupcakes.

Double Chocolate Cupcakes

This cupcake batter is swimming in cocoa and chocolate chips, producing a cupcake that is bursting with chocolate flavor. Use confectioners' sugar on top instead of frosting.

3/4 cup vegetable oil
1 1/4 cups sugar
2 eggs
1 teaspoon vanilla extract
1 3/4 cups all-purpose flour
1/2 cup unsweetened cocoa powder
1 teaspoon baking soda
1/2 teaspoon salt
1 cup milk
1 3/4 cups mini semi-sweet chocolate chips
Confectioners' sugar

In a large bowl, beat vegetable oil and sugar until light and fluffy. Add eggs and vanilla; beat well. Add milk. Mix together flour, cocoa, baking soda and salt. Add flour mixture to shortening mixture; beat well. Add the chocolate chips and mix well.

Fill muffin cups that are lined with paper cupcake liners two-thirds full of batter. Bake in preheated oven at 375 degrees F for 20 to 25 minutes or until cupcake springs back when touched lightly in center. Cool on wire racks. Sprinkle confectioners' sugar over top of cupcakes.

Yield: 24 cupcakes.

Chocolate Zucchini Cupcakes

Using zucchini as an ingredient makes these sweet cupcakes extremely moist and delicious. And no need for frosting.

1/2 cup margarine
1/2 cup vegetable oil
1 3/4 cups sugar
1/2 cup buttermilk
2 eggs
1 teaspoon vanilla
2 1/2 cups flour
1/4 cup unsweetened cocoa powder
1 teaspoon baking powder
1 teaspoon baking soda
1/2 teaspoon cinnamon
1/2 teaspoon cloves
1/2 teaspoon salt
1/4 cup chopped pecans or walnuts
2 cups grated (unpeeled) zucchini
1/2 cup mini chocolate chips
1/2 cup pecans or walnuts

Cream margarine, oil and sugar. Slowly beat in buttermilk, eggs and vanilla. Combine flour, cocoa, baking powder, baking soda, cinnamon, cloves and salt; add to creamed mixture. Add nuts and zucchini. Fill muffin cups lined with paper cupcake liners two-thirds full of batter. Sprinkle chocolate chips and nuts on top. Bake in preheated oven at 325 degrees F for 35 minutes.

Yield: 30 cupcakes.

Chocolate Oatmeal Cupcakes

You can't go wrong with a chocolate oatmeal cupcake with creamy chocolate frosting; they are just that good. Perfect for a tea or coffee break or with a frosty glass of milk.

1 1/2 cups flour
1 teaspoon baking powder
1/2 teaspoon baking soda
1/2 teaspoon salt
1/4 cup butter or margarine, softened
1 cup sugar
2 eggs, beaten
1 teaspoon vanilla extract
1 (3 oz.) unsweetened chocolate, melted and cooled
2/3 cup buttermilk
1/2 cup rolled oats

Combine flour, baking powder, baking soda and salt; set aside. Cream butter and sugar, until fluffy and light; add eggs and vanilla. Stir in chocolate; mix well. Add flour mixture and buttermilk; stir until well blended. Stir in oats. Fill muffin cups lined with paper cupcake liners two-thirds full of batter.

Bake in preheated oven at 375 degrees F for 12 minutes or until inserted toothpick comes out clean. Cool, frost each with 1 tablespoon frosting and top with nut half or skip frosting and nut halves and sprinkle with confectioners' sugar.

Yield: 16 cupcakes.

Creamy Chocolate Frosting for Oatmeal Cupcakes:

2/3 cup evaporated milk
1/2 cup water
2 tablespoons butter or margarine
2 teaspoons cornstarch
1/8 teaspoon salt
1 (6 oz.) package semi-sweet chocolate pieces
1 teaspoon vanilla extract

Over low heat in a small saucepan, cook and stir milk, water, butter or margarine, cornstarch and salt until thickened and smooth; remove from heat. Stir in chocolate until melted, returning to low heat, if necessary. Stir in vanilla. Chill until thickened and of spreading consistency. Store covered in refrigerator. Stir before using.

Yield: 1 1/2 cups.

German Chocolate Cupcakes

These cupcakes with German chocolate and pecans will become a family favorite. The coconut and pecan frosting is absolutely delicious.

4 (1 oz.) squares German sweet chocolate
1 cup margarine
1 1/2 cups chopped pecans
1 3/4 cups sugar
1 cup flour
4 eggs
1 teaspoon vanilla

Melt chocolate and margarine. Add nuts; let cool. Add sugar, flour, eggs, and vanilla. Mix only until well blended. Fill muffin cups lined with paper cupcake liners two-thirds full of batter. Bake in preheated oven for 35 minutes at 350 degrees F.

Coconut Pecan Frosting:

1 cup sugar
1 cup evaporated milk
1/2 cup butter
3 egg yolks, beaten
1 cup pecans, chopped
1 1/3 cups flaked coconut
1 teaspoon vanilla extract
Toasted coconut, optional

In a saucepan, combine sugar, evaporated milk, butter and egg yolks. Cook over low heat, stirring constantly until thickened. Remove from heat. Stir in pecans, coconut and vanilla. Cool frosting until it thickens, then frost cupcakes. Sprinkle with toasted coconut, if desired.

(Note: To toast coconut, bake coconut on a baking sheet in a single layer in a 350 degree oven for 10 minutes, or until just beginning to brown.)

Yield: 20 cupcakes.

Chocolate Cinnamon Cupcakes

These delectable chocolate cupcakes have a subtle cinnamon flavor. Frost with the frosting below or try the Toasted Pecan-Cream Cheese Frosting.

2 cups flour
2 cups sugar
1/2 cup butter or margarine
1/2 cup vegetable oil
6 tablespoons unsweetened cocoa powder
1 cup water
1/2 cup buttermilk
2 teaspoons cinnamon
1 teaspoon vanilla
1 teaspoon baking soda
3 eggs
1 teaspoon salt

Mix flour and sugar. In a saucepan, mix butter or margarine, oil, cocoa, and water; bring to a boil. Pour hot mixture over flour mixture; mix well. Add buttermilk, cinnamon and vanilla. Add baking soda, salt and eggs. Beat until well blended. Fill muffin cups lined with paper cupcake liners two-thirds full of batter. Bake in preheated oven for 15 minutes at 350 degrees F.

Frosting:

1/4 cup butter or margarine, melted
3 tablespoons unsweetened cocoa powder
3 tablespoons buttermilk
1/2 teaspoon vanilla

3 cups confectioners' sugar

Mix frosting ingredients and spread on cooled cupcakes. Add more milk if needed for thinning. Frost and garnish with cinnamon sugar or cocoa.

Yield: 24 cupcakes.

Chocolate Cupcakes

Indulge your chocolate cravings with a chocolate cupcake complete with chocolate frosting. Chocolate cupcakes are also great party food.

Suggested frosting: Chocolate Frosting

1/2 cup butter or margarine, softened
1 cup sugar
1 teaspoon vanilla
4 eggs
1 1/4 cups all-purpose flour
3/4 teaspoon baking soda
1 1/2 cups chocolate syrup

Cream butter or margarine, sugar and vanilla in large mixing bowl until light and fluffy. Add eggs; beat well. Combine flour and baking soda; add alternately with chocolate syrup to creamed mixture. Fill muffin cups that are lined with paper cupcake liners half full of batter.

Bake in preheated oven at 375 degrees F for 15 to 20 minutes or until inserted toothpick comes out clean. Cool; frost as desired.

Yield: 30 cupcakes.

Mini Brownie Cupcakes

These mini brownie cups are small in size but big in taste and will satisfy the most discriminating sweet tooth. Use a muffin tin with cups that are 1 3/4 inch in diameter.

Suggested frosting: Pistachio Buttercream Frosting

1/4 cup margarine
2 egg whites
1 egg
3/4 cup sugar
2/3 cup all-purpose flour
1/3 cup unsweetened cocoa powder
1/4 teaspoon salt
1/2 teaspoon baking powder

In a small saucepan over low heat, melt margarine; cool slightly. In a mixer bowl, on medium speed of electric mixer, beat egg whites and egg until foamy. Add sugar and beat until somewhat thickened.

In a medium bowl, mix together flour, cocoa, salt and baking powder; add to sugar mixture and beat until blended. Gradually add margarine and beat just until mixed well. Fill muffin cups lined with paper cupcake liners two-thirds full of batter. Bake in preheated oven at 350 degrees F for 16 to 18 minutes or until inserted toothpick comes out clean. Cool completely then frost.

Yield: 24 mini cupcakes.

Miscellaneous Cupcakes

Peanut Butter Cupcakes

Add 2/3 cup of chocolate pieces to the top of the cupcakes after removing from oven for a chocolate and peanut butter treat.

Suggested Frosting: Fluffy Frosting or Peanut Butter Glaze

1/2 cup butter
1 1/2 cups brown sugar
1/2 cup peanut butter
1 teaspoon vanilla
2 eggs
1 1/2 cups flour
1/2 teaspoon salt
2/3 cup milk
2 teaspoons baking powder

Combine all ingredients in a large bowl. Beat ingredients with electric mixer on low speed just until blended. Increase speed to high and beat for 2 minutes.

Fill muffin cups that are lined with paper cupcake liners two-thirds full of batter. Bake in preheated oven at 350 degrees F for 25 to 30 minutes or until an inserted toothpick comes out clean.

Yield: 24 cupcakes.

Snickerdoodle Cupcakes

Bursting with the taste of cinnamon and sugar, these mouthwatering cupcakes are like the famous cookie.

1/2 cup butter or margarine
1 cup sugar
1 tablespoon vanilla
2 eggs
2 cups cake flour
2 1/2 tablespoons baking powder
1/2 tablespoon salt
1/2 cup milk

Topping:

3 tablespoons sugar
1 1/2 tablespoons cinnamon
1/2 cup chopped walnuts

Cream butter or margarine and sugar until fluffy. Add vanilla and eggs; beat thoroughly. Combine flour with baking powder and salt. Add to sugar mixture in thirds alternately with milk, beating until smooth after each addition.

Fill muffin cups that are greased or lined with paper cupcake liners one-half full of batter. Mix together ingredients for the topping and sprinkle over batter. Bake in preheated oven at 375 degrees F for 20 minutes or until done.

Yield: 24 cupcakes.

Orange Zucchini Cupcakes

For easy cupcake decorating, put the cream cheese frosting in a resealable bag about halfway full and cut a small hole on the corner of the bag.

1 1/2 cups vegetable oil
1 1/2 cups sugar
3 eggs
1 teaspoon vanilla
1/4 cup orange liqueur
1 1/2 teaspoons grated orange rind
3 cups flour
2 teaspoons cinnamon
2 teaspoons baking soda
1 teaspoon baking powder
3/4 teaspoon salt
2 cups grated zucchini
1 cup chopped walnuts
1 cup finely chopped dates

In a large bowl, beat together oil and sugar with an electric mixer. Add eggs, beating after each egg addition. Add vanilla, liqueur and orange rind. Mix dry ingredients and add to batter. Stir in zucchini, walnuts and dates. Fill muffin cups that are lined with paper cupcake liners half full of batter. Bake in preheated oven at 375 degrees F for 20 to 25 minutes.

Frosting:

1/2 cup softened butter
1 (8 oz.) package soft cream cheese

2 cups confectioners' sugar
2 tablespoons orange liqueur
1 tablespoon grated orange rind
1 teaspoon vanilla

Beat all ingredients together until smooth with electric mixer.
Spread on cooled cupcakes.

Yield: 24 cupcakes.

Root Beer Cupcakes

Root beer concentrate can be found in the spice aisle with the other extracts.

1 cup sugar
1/2 cup margarine or butter
2 eggs
2 teaspoons root beer concentrate
2 cups all-purpose flour
1 tablespoon baking powder
1 teaspoon salt
2/3 cup root beer

In a medium bowl, cream sugar and margarine or butter until fluffy and light. Add root beer concentrate and eggs; beat until well mixed. In another bowl, mix together flour, baking powder and salt. Add the flour mixture to the root beer mixture. Beat in root beer just until combined.

Line muffin cups with paper cupcake liners and fill two-thirds full of batter. Bake in preheated oven at 375 degrees F for 18 to 20 minutes or until inserted toothpick comes out clean. Drizzle with root beer glaze.
Yield: 18 cupcakes.

Root Beer Glaze
4 tablespoons confectioner's sugar
1/4 teaspoon root beer concentrate
Milk, as needed

Mix the sugar and concentrate together adding a teaspoon of milk at a time until desired thinness. Drizzle on cupcakes.

Old-Fashioned Spice Cupcakes

Add a teaspoon of ground cinnamon to the cream cheese frosting on this hearty cupcake for extra spice.

Suggested Frosting: Cream Cheese Frosting

2 cups raisins
2 cups water
1/2 cup vegetable oil
1 1/2 cups sugar
2 eggs
2 1/2 cups flour
1/2 teaspoon cloves
1 teaspoon nutmeg
2 teaspoons cinnamon
1 teaspoon salt
2 1/2 teaspoons baking powder
1 cup chopped nuts

Wash raisins; cover with 2 cups water and simmer gently for 15 minutes. Drain well; cool. Save 1 cup of liquid.

Cream oil; add sugar, cream thoroughly. Add well beaten eggs. Mix flour with cloves, nutmeg, cinnamon, salt and baking powder. Sprinkle 2 tablespoons flour over raisins. Add remaining mixture alternately to the creamed mixture with the liquid. Add raisins and nuts. Fill muffin cups lined with paper cupcake liners two-thirds full of batter. Bake in preheated oven at 350 degrees F for 25 to 30 minutes.

Yield: 24 cupcakes.

Classic Red Velvet

These timeless red velvet cupcakes are fun, easy to make and a hit at every party!

Suggested Frosting: Cream Cheese Frosting

2 cups flour
1/3 cup unsweetened cocoa powder
1/2 teaspoon salt
3/4 teaspoon baking soda
3/4 cup and 2 teaspoons butter, softened
1 3/4 cups sugar
3 eggs
1/3 cup and 1 tablespoon milk
3/4 cup and 2 teaspoons sour cream
3/4 (1 oz.) bottle red food coloring
1 1/2 teaspoons vanilla extract

In a bowl, combine flour, cocoa powder, salt and baking soda; set aside. With an electric mixer, beat butter and sugar in a large bowl for 5 minutes on medium speed. Add the eggs, one at a time, beating after each addition. Mix in milk, sour cream, food coloring and vanilla. Slowly add flour mixture, beating on low speed until just blended. Fill muffin cups lined with paper cupcake liners two-thirds full of batter.

Bake in preheated oven at 350 degrees F for 20 minutes or until inserted toothpick comes out clean. Cool in pans for 5 minutes, then remove.

Yield: 24 cupcakes.

Black Bottom Cupcakes

These rich and gooey black bottom cupcakes with a great cream cheese surprise are so good.

1 1/2 cups flour
1/4 cup unsweetened cocoa powder
1/2 teaspoon salt
1 teaspoon baking soda
1/3 cup vegetable oil
1 cup sugar
1 cup water
1 teaspoon vanilla
1 teaspoon white vinegar

Mix together flour, cocoa, salt and baking soda; set aside. Cream oil and sugar together. Add dry mixture and mix well. Add water, vanilla and vinegar. Blend well. Fill muffin cups lined with paper cupcake liners one-half full of batter. Add 1 teaspoon topping on each. Bake in preheated oven at 350 degrees F for 20 minutes.

Yield: 24 cupcakes.

Topping for Cupcakes
1 (8 oz.) package cream cheese
1 egg
1/3 cup sugar
1/8 teaspoon salt
1 (6 oz.) mini chocolate chips

Add sugar, egg and salt to softened cream cheese. Blend well. Stir in chocolate chips. Spoon topping as directed.

Cupcakes with Vanilla and Chocolate Frostings

These yummy cupcakes have the best of both worlds with vanilla and chocolate frosting. A quick and easy way to frost cupcakes is to dip cupcakes into frosting and turn slightly to coat.

1 large egg
1 1/2 cups flour
1 cup sugar
1/2 cup buttermilk
1/2 cup unsweetened cocoa powder
1/2 cup unsalted butter, softened
1/2 cup hot water
1 teaspoon baking soda
1 teaspoon vanilla extract
1/2 teaspoon salt

Combine all the cupcake ingredients in a bowl. Beat with an electric mixer until smooth. Fill muffin cups that are lined with paper cupcake liners two-thirds full of batter. Bake in preheated oven at 350 degrees F 20 to 25 or until an inserted toothpick comes out clean.

Chocolate and Vanilla Frostings

3 cups confectioners' sugar
4 tablespoons unsalted butter, softened
3 tablespoons unsweetened cocoa powder (optional for vanilla frosting)
2 tablespoons buttermilk

2 tablespoons whole milk
1 teaspoon vanilla extract
1/8 teaspoon salt

In a large bowl, combine all the ingredients, adding cocoa powder for chocolate frosting or eliminating the cocoa powder for vanilla frosting. With an electric mixer, beat until creamy and smooth. Using about 2 tablespoons per cupcake, spread vanilla or chocolate frosting on each.

If desired, place toppings on separate plates and dip the cupcakes into toppings. Toppings to use include colored sugar, candy coated chocolates, mini chocolate chips, multicolored or chocolate sprinkles, or nuts.

Yield: 16 cupcakes.

Carrot Cupcakes

It's mandatory to use the cream cheese frosting on these carrot cake cupcakes!

4 eggs
2 cups sugar
1 1/4 cups vegetable oil
2 cups flour
2 teaspoons allspice
2 teaspoons cinnamon
2 teaspoons baking soda
1/2 teaspoon salt
2 cups carrots, grated
1 cup seedless raisins
1 cup chopped walnuts or pecans

Beat together eggs, sugar and oil. Mix together flour, allspice, cinnamon, baking soda and salt; add to egg mixture. Beat well. Add carrots, raisins and walnuts or pecans.

Fill muffin cups lined with paper cupcake liners two-thirds full of batter. Bake in preheated oven at 350 degrees F for 15 to 20 minutes or until toothpick inserted in center comes out clean.

Yield: 24 cupcakes.

Apricot Coffee Cupcakes

Enjoy the sweet taste of apricots in these delectable cupcakes with confectioners' sugar icing.

1 cup sugar
4 eggs
1 teaspoon vanilla
1/4 teaspoon almond extract
1 cup vegetable oil
2 cups all-purpose flour
1 teaspoon baking powder
1/2 teaspoon salt
1 (21 oz.) can apricot pie filling

Beat eggs until fluffy. Add sugar gradually, beat until thick. Blend in vanilla, almond extract and oil. Add flour, baking powder and salt. Spread half of batter in greased or paper-lined muffin tins. Spoon on pie filling. Carefully spread on rest of the batter. Bake in preheated oven at 350 degrees F for 20 minutes. While warm, drizzle with confectioners' sugar icing.

Confectioners' Sugar Icing
1 cup confectioners' sugar
1/2 teaspoon vanilla
1 to 2 tablespoons milk

Mix and spread on cooled cupcakes. Add more milk if needed for thinning.

Yield: 15 cupcakes.

No Frost Cupcakes

You won't miss the frosting with a cupcake as moist and delicious as this one.

1 (8 oz.) package cream cheese, softened
1/3 cup sugar
1 egg
1/8 teaspoon salt
1 (6 oz.) package chocolate chips
1 1/2 cups flour
1 cup sugar
1 teaspoon baking soda
1/4 cup unsweetened cocoa powder
1 cup water
1/2 teaspoon salt
1/3 cup vegetable oil
1 tablespoon white vinegar
1 teaspoon vanilla

In a medium bowl, mix together first 4 ingredients. Stir in chocolate chips. In another bowl, mix together remaining ingredients. Fill muffin cups that are lined with paper cupcake liners 1/3 full with flour mixture. Add heaping teaspoon of cream cheese mixture. Bake in preheated oven at 350 degrees F for 25 to 30 minutes.

Yield: 24 cupcakes.

Swanny Cream Cheese Delights

Adding a dollop of fruit changes a cupcake into a healthy food, right? A batch of these delectable cupcakes won't last long.

3 (8 oz.) packages cream cheese, softened
1 cup sugar
5 eggs
1 1/2 teaspoons vanilla
1 (8 oz.) container sour cream
1/4 cup sugar
1 jar fruit preserves

Blend cream cheese with 1 cup sugar. Mix in eggs, one at a time. Add vanilla. Fill muffin cups that are lined with paper cupcake liners 1/2 full of batter. Bake in preheated oven for 35 to 40 minutes at 350 degrees F.

Combine sour cream with 1/4 cup sugar. While still warm, spoon 1 tablespoon of sour cream mixture over each cupcake. Add a dab of fruit preserves on each. Bake 5 minutes more. Refrigerate.

Yield: 24 cupcakes.

Shoofly Cupcakes

Shoofly Cupcakes are a variation of Shoofly Pie, an old Pennsylvania Dutch molasses pie with a yummy crumb topping.

1 cup vegetable oil
1 cup sugar
2 eggs, well beaten
1 cup dark molasses
1 teaspoon baking soda, dissolved in
1 cup lukewarm water
3 cups flour

Crumb Topping:

1/2 cup flour
1/4 cup sugar
1/4 cup butter

Cream oil; gradually add sugar. Beat until light and fluffy. Add eggs, blending well. In a small bowl, dissolve baking soda in 1 cup warm water; add molasses. Slowly add to creamed mixture. Add flour; mix well.

Mix ingredients for crumb topping together with a pastry blender until crumbly. Fill muffin cups lined with paper cupcake liners two-thirds full of batter. Top with 1 tablespoon crumb topping. Bake in preheated oven at 350 degrees F for 30 to 35 minutes.

Yield: 12 cupcakes.

Chocolate Flake Cupcakes

These cupcakes will stick to cupcake papers if used, so go with greasing or spraying the muffin pan cups with non-stick cooking spray instead of using papers. (or at least spray the papers with cooking spray.) A good frosting for these is a simple confectioners' sugar icing – 1 cup confectioners' sugar, 1/2 teaspoon vanilla and 1 to 2 tablespoons milk. Just mix and spread on cooled cupcakes.

4 squares (1 oz.) semi-sweet chocolate
1 cup margarine
1 cup pecans
1 3/4 cups sugar
1 cup flour
4 eggs
1 teaspoon vanilla
1/8 teaspoon salt

Melt chocolate and margarine. Add pecans. Mix by hand, sugar, flour, eggs, vanilla and salt with chocolate mixture until blended. Fill greased muffin cups two-thirds full of batter. Bake in preheated oven at 325 degrees F for 35 minutes.

Yield: 18 cupcakes.

Lemon Cupcakes

To make a filled lemon cupcake, add a spoonful of vanilla pudding in the middle of each cupcake before frosting them.

Suggested Frosting: Lemon-flavored Frosting

2 cups all-purpose flour
2 teaspoons baking powder
1/4 teaspoon salt
1 1/3 cups white sugar
2/3 cup unsalted butter
3 eggs
3/4 teaspoon vanilla extract
2 tablespoons lemon zest
2/3 cup whole milk, divided
2 tablespoons fresh lemon juice, divided

In a bowl, combine flour and salt. In another bowl, with an electric mixer, cream the sugar and butter until fluffy and light. Beat in eggs, one at a time. Mix in lemon zest and vanilla extract.

Add half the flour mixture to the sugar mixture and beat just until combined. Add half the milk and half of the lemon juice and beat. Beat in the remaining half of the flour mixture, then the remaining half of the milk and lemon juice, just until well combined.

Fill muffin cups that are lined with paper cupcake liners 3/4 full with batter. Bake in preheated oven at 375 degrees F about 17 minutes or until a toothpick inserted in the center comes out clean. Let the cupcakes cool in the pans for about

10 minutes before removing them to finish cooling on a rack. Refrigerate leftovers.

Yield: 20 cupcakes.

Devil's Dump Cupcakes

Make an easy dump cake in the form of cupcakes. Nuts are optional.

Suggested frosting: Toasted Pecan Frosting

1 1/2 cups flour
1/2 cup unsweetened cocoa powder
1 cup sugar
2 1/2 teaspoons baking powder
1/8 teaspoon baking soda
1/8 teaspoon salt
1 cup cold water
2/3 cup oil
1 teaspoon vanilla
2 eggs

Combine flour, cocoa, sugar, baking powder, baking soda and salt; make a well in center. Add water, oil, vanilla and eggs. Beat well with beater. Fill muffin cups lined with paper cupcake liners two-thirds full of batter. Bake in preheated oven at 350 degrees F for 20 minutes or until toothpick comes out clean. Cool on cooling rack and then frost.

Yield: 18 cupcakes.

Applesauce Cupcakes

Using applesauce in place of butter make these cupcakes a healthier treat option.

Suggested Frosting: Pineapple-Cream Cheese Frosting

1 cup sugar
1/2 cup vegetable oil
1 egg
1 cup applesauce
1 1/2 cups flour
1/2 teaspoon cinnamon
1/2 teaspoon nutmeg
1/4 teaspoon salt
1 teaspoon baking soda dissolved in 1 tablespoon hot water
1/2 cup chopped raisins and nuts

Mix ingredients together in order given. Fill muffin cups lined with paper cupcake liners two-thirds full of batter. Bake in preheated oven at 350 degrees F for 20 minutes or until toothpick inserted in center comes out clean.

Yield: 24 cupcakes.

Kid Pleasin' Cupcakes

These stir and bake cupcakes don't require a mixer, so they go together super quick.

Suggested Frosting: Pistachio Frosting

1 (4 oz.) package instant pistachio pudding mix
1 3/4 cups flour
3/4 cup mini chocolate chips
2/3 cup sugar
1/2 teaspoon salt
2 1/2 teaspoons baking powder
1 1/4 cups milk
1/2 cup vegetable oil
1 teaspoon vanilla extract
2 eggs, beaten
1/2 cup candy coated milk chocolate pieces

In a large bowl, combine pudding mix, flour, chocolate chips, sugar, salt and baking powder. In a small bowl, mix together milk, oil, vanilla and eggs. Stir into flour mixture just until well mixed.

Fill muffin cups lined with paper cupcake liners two-thirds full of batter. Bake in a preheated 375 degrees F oven for 18 to 20 minutes or until golden brown. Cool and frost. Sprinkle with milk chocolate pieces.

Yield: 18 cupcakes.

Cracker Jack Cupcakes

Enjoy melted butter and brown sugar poured on top of a tasty cupcake filled with crunchy peanut candy.

Simple White or Yellow cupcake recipe
16 oz. Cracker Jacks, crushed
1/2 cup butter
1 cup brown sugar
1/4 cup milk
3 tablespoons milk
1 3/4 cups confectioners' sugar

Prepare batter for either the Simple White Cupcakes or Simple Yellow Cupcakes in this recipe book. Pour batter into cupcake tins, then sprinkle crushed Cracker Jacks on top. Bake as directed in cupcake recipe. Remove from oven and before cupcakes have cooled, pour the following topping over the top. No need to spread it; it will fill in the nooks and crannies perfectly.

Topping:

Melt butter in saucepan and stir in brown sugar. Stir and boil over medium heat for 2 minutes. Stir in 1/4 cup milk and bring to boil, stirring constantly. Cool until lukewarm; add 3 tablespoons of milk. Gradually add confectioner's sugar, stirring until desired consistency is obtained. Add more milk if needed.

Yield: 24 cupcakes

Banana Apple Cupcakes

Just as with banana bread, be sure the banana is ripe with black or brown spots on the skins, for a sweet banana flavor.

1 cup all-purpose flour
1/2 teaspoon salt
1/2 teaspoon baking soda
1/4 teaspoon ground nutmeg
1/4 teaspoon ground cinnamon
1/3 cup shortening
1/2 cup and 2 tablespoons sugar
1 egg
2 tablespoons buttermilk
1/2 teaspoon vanilla extract
1/2 cup ripe bananas, mashed
1 apple

Core, peel and shred the apple; set aside. In a large bowl, combine flour, salt, baking soda, nutmeg and cinnamon. In another bowl, cream together shortening and sugar until fluffy and light. Beat in the egg; add buttermilk and vanilla. Add flour mixture, beating just until flour is moistened. Fold in the apples and bananas.

Fill muffin cups lined with paper cupcake liners one-half full of batter. Bake in preheated oven at 375 degrees F for 20 to 25 minutes.

Yield: 12 cupcakes.

Nutty Cranberry Cupcakes

Chewy delicious cranberries coupled with the crunch of tasty nuts will make these cupcakes a family favorite.

1 1/4 cups sugar
1 1/2 cups frozen cranberries
1/2 cup softened butter
2 large eggs
2 teaspoons vanilla
2 cups all-purpose flour
4 teaspoons baking powder
1 teaspoon sweet lemonade drink mix
1/2 teaspoon salt
1 cup milk
1 cup chopped walnuts
Cream cheese frosting

Chop thawed cranberries and divide sugar. Put cranberries and 1/4 cup of sugar in small bowl and mix together well. Cream together butter and the remaining sugar in a large mixing bowl. To the butter mixture add eggs one at a time beating batter after each egg is added. Beat in the vanilla extract. In a separate bowl mix together the baking powder, flour, lemonade drink mix and salt; add this to butter mixture alternately with the milk. Fold in the nuts and cranberries.

Fill muffin cups lined with paper cupcake liners two-thirds full of batter. Bake in preheated 400 degree F oven for 12 to 17 minutes; toothpick should come out clean when done. Let cupcakes cool for five minutes in pan then be placed on wire rack to cool throughout. Spread frosting on each cupcake. Yield: 24 cupcakes.

Gingerbread Cupcakes

Doesn't have to be Christmas to enjoy a spicy gingerbread cupcake in the morning!

2 1/2 cups all-purpose flour
1/4 cup cornstarch
1 teaspoon baking soda
1 teaspoon baking powder
1 tablespoon ground ginger
1 teaspoon ground cinnamon
1/2 teaspoon salt
1/2 teaspoon ground allspice
1 cup milk
3 large eggs
2 teaspoons vanilla extract
1 cup molasses
1 cup unsalted butter, room temperature
1 cup brown sugar

In a large bowl, mix together flour, cornstarch, baking soda and baking powder. Add ginger, cinnamon, salt and allspice. In another bowl, combine milk, eggs, vanilla extract and molasses.

With an electric mixer, beat butter into dry ingredients, first on low, then medium, until mixture resembles small pebbles. Mix in 1/3 of the molasses mixture; beat on low speed until mixture is smooth. While beating on medium speed, add the rest of the milk mixture in two phases and beat until batter is smooth. Mix in the brown sugar; beat for 30 seconds until just combined well.

Fill muffin cups lined with paper cupcake liners two-thirds full of batter. Bake in preheated oven for 15 to 20 minutes in 350 degrees F oven or until an inserted toothpick comes out clean.

Yield: 24 cupcakes.

Orange Cupcakes

A single orange comes together with raisins and nuts in this cupcake.

1 cup sugar
1/2 cup butter
2 eggs
1 cup raisins (ground)
2 cups flour
1/2 cup nuts, finely chopped
2/3 cup sour cream
1 orange (juice and rind, ground)
1 teaspoon vanilla
1 teaspoon baking soda

Reserve about 2 teaspoons raisins, orange and nuts for frosting, then combine all the rest of the above ingredients. Fill muffin cups lined with paper cupcake liners two-thirds full of batter. Bake in preheated oven at 350 degrees F for 20 minutes.

Frosting:
6 tablespoons brown sugar
4 tablespoons butter
2 cups confectioners' sugar

Bring brown sugar and butter to a boil and add confectioners' sugar. Add the reserved raisins, orange and nuts; mix well and frost cupcakes.

Yield: 24 cupcakes.

Choco-Dot Pumpkin Cupcakes

These rich and spicy pumpkin cupcakes don't even need frosting.

2 cups sugar
2 cups flour
1 teaspoon baking soda
2 teaspoons baking powder
1/2 teaspoon salt
1 1/2 teaspoons cinnamon
1/2 teaspoon ground cloves
1/4 teaspoon allspice
1/4 teaspoon ginger
4 eggs
1 cup vegetable oil
1 cup All-Bran cereal
1 1/2 cups pumpkin
1 cup chocolate chips
1 cup walnuts, chopped
Confectioners' sugar (opt.)

*Can substitute 1 cup applesauce for 1 cup of vegetable oil.

Mix together sugar, flour, baking powder, baking soda, salt, cinnamon, cloves, allspice, and ginger. Beat eggs until light and foamy. Add pumpkin, oil and bran. Mix well. Add dry ingredients; mix until combined. Stir in chocolate chips and nuts. Fill muffin cups lined with paper cupcake liners 3/4 full of batter and, in a preheated oven, bake at 350 degrees F for 30 minutes. No frosting needed but, if desired, dust with confectioners' sugar.
Yield: 30 cupcakes.

Strawberry Shortcake Cupcakes

Spread some "Fluffy Frosting" from the frosting category on top of these delicious cupcakes and then top with a strawberry. Or just use whipping cream to frost.

2 1/4 cups all-purpose flour
2 tablespoons white sugar
4 teaspoons baking powder
1/4 teaspoon salt
1/3 cup shortening
2/3 cup milk
1 egg, well beaten
1 cup fresh strawberries, diced
6 strawberries, cut in half to be placed on top

In a bowl, mix together flour, sugar, baking powder and salt. With a pastry blender, cut in shortening until the mixture is similar to coarse crumbs. Add milk and egg; mix just until moistened. Fold in diced strawberries.

Fill muffin cups lined with paper cupcake liners 3/4 full of batter. Bake in a preheated oven at 425 degrees F for 12 to 15 minutes. Let cupcakes cool throughout on wire rack before frosting. Place a half strawberry on the top of each frosted cupcake.

Yield: 12 cupcakes.

Vegan Cupcakes

Awesome cupcakes, even if you aren't vegan! If coconut oil is not available, canola oil can be substituted. Also lemon juice can be substituted for the apple cider vinegar.

1 tablespoon and 1 teaspoon apple cider vinegar
2 cups soy milk or almond milk
2 2/3 cups all-purpose flour
1 1/3 cups white sugar (or vegan cane sugar)
2 3/4 teaspoons baking powder
3/4 teaspoon salt
3/4 teaspoon baking soda
2/3 cup coconut oil
1 3/4 teaspoons vanilla extract

Measure the apple cider vinegar into a 2 cup measuring cup. Add soy or almond milk to make 2 cups. Let stand 5 minutes or until curdled.

In a large bowl, combine flour, sugar, baking powder, salt and baking soda. In a microwave, heat the coconut oil on 1/2 power until it is totally liquid. In another bowl, combine soy milk mixture, coconut oil and vanilla; mix well. Add the wet ingredients to the flour mixture; mix just until well combined. Fill muffin cups lined with paper cupcake liners two-thirds full of batter. Bake in preheated oven at 350 degrees F for 15 to 20 minutes or until inserted toothpick comes out clean. When cool, frost with coconut frosting.

Yield: 24 cupcakes.

Coconut Frosting for Vegan Cupcakes

1 cup powdered sugar
1 cup coconut
1 tablespoon coconut oil
1/4 cup almond milk

Combine frosting ingredients in a saucepan and bring to a boil. Boil for 5 minutes. Spread frosting on cupcakes while the frosting is warm.

Simple White Cupcakes

Add mini chocolate chips in the frosting to dress up these simple and easy cupcakes. These cupcakes would also be a hit at a wedding.

Suggested Frosting: Buttercream Frosting

2 cups flour
1 1/2 cups sugar
1 cup milk
1/2 cup butter
3 1/2 teaspoons baking powder
1 teaspoon vanilla
1 teaspoon salt
4 egg whites

In a large bowl, mix flour, sugar, milk, butter, baking powder, vanilla and salt. With electric mixer, beat for 30 seconds at low speed. Beat 2 minutes on high. Add the egg whites and beat for 2 minutes.

Fill muffin cups lined with paper cupcake liners two-thirds full of batter. Bake in preheated oven at 350 degrees F for 15 to 20 minutes or until inserted toothpick comes out clean.

Yield: 24 cupcakes.

Simple Yellow Cupcakes

A simple from-scratch delicious yellow cupcake - plain, moist and easy to make.

2/3 cup margarine, softened
2 eggs
1 3/4 cups sugar
1 1/2 teaspoons vanilla
2 3/4 cups flour
2 1/2 teaspoons baking powder
1 teaspoon salt
1 1/4 cups milk

In a large bowl, cream margarine, eggs, sugar and vanilla with electric mixer until light and fluffy. In another bowl, combine flour, baking powder and salt; add alternately with milk to wet ingredients. Beat to a soft smooth batter.

Fill muffin cups lined with paper cupcake liners two-thirds full of batter. Bake in preheated oven at 350 degrees F for 15 to 20 minutes or until inserted toothpick comes out clean.

Yield: 30 cupcakes.

Filled Cupcakes

S'more Cupcakes

You don't need a campfire to enjoy the taste of s'mores; just place the gooey marshmallow treat mixture in the center of a cupcake.

2/3 cup vegetable oil
1 1/2 cups sugar
3 large eggs
1 1/2 cups graham cracker crumbs
1 1/2 cups all-purpose flour
2 teaspoons baking powder
1 teaspoon salt
1 1/4 cups milk
1 teaspoon vanilla extract
24 chocolate kisses, removed from foil
4 cups miniature marshmallows

With an electric mixer, beat vegetable oil at medium speed. Add sugar gradually, mixing well. Add eggs, 1 at a time, beating after each addition. In another bowl, combine graham cracker crumbs, flour, baking powder and salt; add flour mixture to sugar mixture alternately with milk. Beat until well mixed after each addition. Stir in vanilla.

Fill muffin cups lined with paper cupcake liners with 1/4 cup of batter in each cup. Bake in preheated oven at 350 degrees F for 18 minutes or until done. Immediately imbed a chocolate kiss in the center of each cupcake; followed by 4 or 5 marshmallows, gently pushing into the soft chocolate.

Yield: 24 cupcakes.

Crème-Filled Cupcakes

This recipe may be a little time-consuming but this yummy cupcake filled with a surprise crème in the center is worth it.

3/4 cup vegetable oil
1 1/4 cups sugar
2 eggs
1 teaspoon vanilla
1 3/4 cups all-purpose flour
1/2 cup unsweetened cocoa powder
1 teaspoon baking soda
1/2 teaspoon salt
1 cup milk
Crème filling (recipe below)

Cream vegetable oil and sugar in large mixing bowl. Add eggs and vanilla; blend well. In another bowl, mix together flour, cocoa, baking soda and salt; add alternately with milk to sugar mixture. Fill muffin cups lined with paper liners two-thirds full of batter. Bake in preheated oven at 375 degrees F for 20 to 25 minutes or until inserted toothpick comes out clean. Cool completely.

Prepare crème filling; spoon into pastry bag with open star tip. Insert the tip into center of top of cupcake; lightly squeeze until cupcake is full. Cover top with swirl of filling.

Yield: 24 cupcakes.

Crème Filling

1/2 cup milk
1/4 cup all-purpose flour

1/4 cup vegetable oil
1/4 cup butter or margarine, softened
2 teaspoons vanilla
1/4 teaspoon salt
4 cups confectioners' sugar

Mix milk and flour together in a small saucepan. Stirring constantly with a wire whisk, cook over low heat until mixture thickens and begins to boil. Remove from heat; chill in refrigerator. Cream vegetable oil and butter in large mixing bowl; add cooled flour mixture, vanilla and salt. Gradually add confectioners' sugar; beat until smooth and creamy.

Frosting:

1/3 cup margarine, melted
1/3 cup brown sugar
1/3 cup cocoa
1/3 cup milk
Confectioners' sugar

Mix frosting ingredients and spread on cooled cupcakes. Add more milk if needed for thinning.

Filled Chocolate Chip Cupcakes

These awesome cupcakes are filled in the center with the deliciousness of chocolate and cream cheese.

3 cups flour
2 cups sugar
2 teaspoons baking soda
1 teaspoon salt
1/2 cup unsweetened cocoa powder
2/3 cup vegetable oil
2 cups cold water
2 tablespoons vinegar
2 teaspoons vanilla

Combine flour, sugar, baking soda, salt, and cocoa. Add vegetable oil, water, vinegar and vanilla and beat until smooth. Fill muffin cups lined with paper cupcake liners over half full of batter. Place 1 teaspoon filling on top of each.

Filling:

1 (8 oz.) package cream cheese, softened
1 egg
1/3 cup sugar
3/4 cup caramel or chocolate chips
1/4 teaspoon black walnut flavoring

To make filling:

Combine cream cheese, egg, and sugar; add caramel or chocolate chips and flavoring.

Bake cupcakes in preheated oven at 350 degrees for 25 minutes. Frost when cool.

Frosting:

4 cups confectioners' sugar
1 tablespoon butter
1 to 2 tablespoons unsweetened cocoa powder
Milk

Mix sugar and butter, add cocoa and blend well. Add enough milk to spread easily.

Yield: 30 cupcakes.

Decorated Cupcakes

Holiday Cupcakes

This cupcake recipe is perfect for the holidays with tasty dates, nuts and chocolate chips. The dates supply a natural sweetening so less sugar is needed for the recipe.

Suggested Frosting: Peppermint Frosting

1 cup hot water
1 cup chopped dates
1 teaspoon baking soda
1 cup sugar
1/2 cup vegetable oil
1 egg
1/2 teaspoon salt
1 teaspoon vanilla
2 cups flour
1/2 cup chocolate chips
1/2 cup chopped nuts (optional)

Combine hot water, dates and baking soda. Let cool. Mix sugar and oil; add to date mixture. Add egg, salt, vanilla and flour to mixture; mix well. Add chocolate chips and nuts. Fill muffin cups lined with paper cupcake liners two-thirds full of

batter. Bake in preheated oven at 350 degrees F for 30 to 35 minutes.
Yield: 24 cupcakes.

Reindeer Cupcakes

Gather the kids into the kitchen and start making these adorable reindeer cupcakes for the holidays. First, bake the cupcakes, choosing from a recipe in the Chocolate Cupcakes category. Then make the Creamy Chocolate Frosting or if you are short on time, a chocolate ready-to-spread frosting will also work.

12 pre-made chocolate cupcakes
Chocolate frosting
Chocolate sprinkles
24 pecan halves
24 pretzel sticks
12 red gumdrops
24 small white breath mints

Frost cupcakes with chocolate frosting, piling high to form a rounded top. Coat frosting with chocolate sprinkles. Insert 2 pecans to form ears and 2 pretzels sticking straight up to form antlers on each. Place a mint in front of each pecan ear to form the eyes. Add a gumdrop to each cupcake for nose. Refrigerate to set frosting.

(Note: Eyes could also be made of flattened mini-marshmallows with a chocolate chip in the center. A mini vanilla wafer for the nose with an attached red M&M would be a nose variation.)

Yield: 12 cupcakes.

Minion Cupcakes

12 Twinkies
White frosting tube
Black frosting tube

Bake *Simple White Cupcakes.* Frost each with *Buttercream Frosting* or a container of ready-made vanilla frosting. Cut each twinkie in half. Lay twinkies on parchment paper or a plate on the twinkie flat side.

Referring to photo, with the black frosting tube, draw lines for glasses and add a mouth. With the white frosting tube, squeeze 2 circles of frosting inside the glasses for the whites of the minion's eyes. Add a black frosting dot in the center of the white. Gently press the twinkie into the frosting cut side down.

Optional - Use chocolate sprinkles for hair, if desired. Can also be made with just one larger eye.

Yield: 12 cupcakes.

Peppermint Candy Cupcakes

These candy topped cupcakes are full of Christmas cheer.

Suggested Frosting: Peppermint Frosting or purchase 2 containers of whipped white frosting.

2 cups sifted flour
1 1/2 cups sugar
3 1/2 teaspoons baking powder
1 teaspoon salt
1/2 cup vegetable oil
1 cup milk
1 teaspoon vanilla
4 egg whites
1 teaspoon peppermint extract
1 teaspoon red paste food coloring
1 cup peppermint hard candies, crushed

In a large bowl, combine flour, sugar, baking powder, salt, vegetable oil, milk and vanilla. With an electric mixer, beat for 30 seconds on low speed. Beat 2 minutes on high. Add egg whites and peppermint extract and beat 2 minutes.

Place half the batter into another bowl. Add the food coloring to one of the halves and mix until well blended. Line 12 muffin cups with paper cupcake liners. Place two tablespoons of the red batter into each muffin cup, top with two tablespoons of the white batter. Using a butter knife, swirl together the white and red batter to produce a marbled look.

Bake in a preheated 350 degree F oven for 18 to 20 minutes. Inserted toothpick should come out clean. Let cupcakes cool for at least ten minutes then remove from pan. Cupcakes should be completely cooled in about thirty minutes. Swirl frosting onto each cupcake and top with crushed peppermints.

Yield: 12 cupcakes.

Santa Claus Cupcakes

Santa never looked as good as he does on these Christmas cupcakes.

Suggested Frosting: Buttercream Frosting

Cupcakes:

2 cups flour
1 1/2 cups sugar
1 cup milk
1/2 cup butter
3 1/2 teaspoons baking powder
1 teaspoon vanilla
1 teaspoon salt
4 egg whites

Decorating:

24 red cinnamon candies, for nose
48 chocolate chips, for eyes
1 1/2 cups white miniature marshmallows
Red decorator sugar
Vanilla frosting

In a large bowl, mix flour, sugar, milk, butter, baking powder, vanilla and salt. With electric mixer, beat for 30 seconds at low speed. Beat 2 minutes on high. Add the egg whites and beat for 2 minutes.

Fill muffin cups lined with paper cupcake liners two-thirds full of batter. Bake at 350 degrees F for 15 to 20 minutes or until inserted toothpick comes out clean. Let cupcakes cool for approximately 30 minutes then spread vanilla frosting on each one. (see Buttercream Frosting)

To make Santa's hat, sprinkle 1/8 teaspoon of the red decorator sugar over the top 1/3 of each cupcake. For Santa's face use two chocolate chips for his eyes and one cinnamon candy for his nose. Cut two marshmallows down the center lengthwise to form the rim of the hat. To make the beard cut four marshmallows down the center crosswise then cover the lower part of the cupcake.

Alternately, just use decorator frosting in red and white to decorate as in photo, still using chocolate chips for eyes. They're cute either way!

Yield: 24 cupcakes.

Frosting & Fillings

Buttercream Frosting

Create this ideal buttercream frosting with just a few ingredients.

1 1/2 cups butter

1 (16 oz.) package confectioners' sugar

2 tablespoons milk

1 teaspoon vanilla extract

With an electric mixer, beat butter at medium speed until creamy; gradually add sugar, creaming until fluffy and light. Add milk and vanilla, beating to desired consistency.

Yield: about 4 cups.

Cacao Chocolate Buttercream Frosting

This creamy chocolate frosting turns a good cupcake into a wonderful cupcake.

1 (4 oz.) cacao bittersweet chocolate baking bar

1/2 cup butter, softened

1/4 teaspoon vanilla

1 1/3 cups confectioners' sugar

Break the baking bar into small pieces and microwave the chocolate on HIGH for 30 seconds. Stir chocolate and if not completely melted, microwave for 10 to 15 more seconds. Repeat with 10 second intervals until melted. Let cool.

In a medium bowl, beat butter and vanilla until fluffy and light. Beat in chocolate until well blended. Add sugar and beat until fluffy and light again. Add one teaspoon of milk at a time until desired consistency.

Yield: 1 1/2 cups.

Cherry Pecan Cream Cheese Frosting

This awesome cream cheese frosting has cherries and pecans.

1 (8 oz.) package cream cheese, softened

1/2 cup butter or margarine, softened

1 teaspoon vanilla extract

1/2 teaspoon coconut extract

1 (16 oz.) package confectioners' sugar

1 cup chopped pecans

1/2 cup chopped maraschino cherries, drained

With an electric mixer, beat cream cheese and butter or margarine in a mixing bowl at medium speed until creamy; add vanilla and coconut extract. Gradually add confectioners' sugar, beating well. Fold in pecans and maraschino cherries.

Yield: 4 1/2 cups.

Pistachio Buttercream Frosting

1 cup unsalted butter, softened

4 cups confectioner's sugar

1.7 oz. pistachio instant pudding mix (1/2 of 3.5-oz. package)

1 1/2 teaspoons vanilla

1/4 teaspoon salt

1/2 cup heavy whipping cream

Beat butter and sugar in medium mixer bowl until light and fluffy. Add instant pudding, vanilla and salt and beat well. Add heavy cream as needed while mixing, until frosting is creamy and fluffy.

Yield: about 3 cups.

Creamy Chocolate Frosting

This smooth and creamy topping may become your favorite chocolate frosting.

1/2 cup butter or margarine, melted

1/3 cup unsweetened cocoa powder

1/3 cup evaporated milk

1 teaspoon vanilla extract

1 (16 oz.) package confectioners' sugar

In a large bowl, combine all ingredients. With an electric mixer, beat at medium speed until well combined. Beat at high speed until mixture reaches spreading consistency. Small amounts of milk may be added to thin, if necessary.

Yield: 2 1/2 cups.

Chocolate Frosting

Give your cupcakes the perfect taste of rich chocolate with this recipe.

1 cup semi-sweet chocolate chips

1 (14 oz.) can sweetened condensed milk

1/8 teaspoon salt

2 cups confectioners' sugar

1 teaspoon vanilla extract

In a medium saucepan, mix together chocolate chips, condensed milk and salt. Cook and stir on medium heat until chocolate chips melt; cook and stir 3 minutes more. Remove from heat; let cool for 15 minutes. With electric mixer on medium, beat in confectioners' sugar and vanilla extract until smooth and creamy.

Yield: about 1 1/2 cups.

Light Chocolate Frosting

Here's a reduced fat chocolate frosting that is still delicious.

1/2 cup 2% low fat cottage cheese

1/4 cup soft margarine

1/4 cup unsweetened cocoa powder

1/4 teaspoon vanilla extract

2 cups confectioners' sugar

In a blender, blend cottage cheese and margarine until smooth. In small mixing bowl, combine cottage cheese mixture, cocoa and vanilla. Gradually beat in confectioners' sugar. Keep frosting refrigerated until use.

Yield: 1 1/2 cups.

Fluffy Frosting

This yummy frosting goes well with almost any type of cupcake and the fluffy texture makes it easy to work with.

1 cup sugar

1/4 teaspoon cream of tartar

1/3 cup water

2 egg whites

1 teaspoon vanilla extract

In a medium saucepan, mix together sugar, cream of tartar, and water. Cook and stir constantly on medium heat until clear. Without stirring, cook to soft ball stage (235 to 240 degrees). With electric mixer, beat egg whites until soft peaks form; continue beating, adding syrup in a slow, steady stream. Add the vanilla; continue beating until stiff peaks form and frosting is thick and creamy.

Yield: 4 cups.

Mocha Buttercream Frosting

Mocha frosting with its wonderful coffee flavor is perfect for a chocolate cupcake.

1 tablespoon instant coffee granules

1/4 cup hot water

1/2 cup butter or margarine, softened

3 tablespoons cocoa

4 1/4 to 4 1/2 cups confectioners' sugar

3/4 teaspoon vanilla extract

Dissolve coffee granules in hot water; set aside to cool. Cream butter or margarine and cocoa on medium speed of an electric mixer; add 4 1/4 cups confectioners' sugar to creamed mixture alternately with coffee, beginning and ending with confectioners' sugar. Add additional 1/4 cup confectioners' sugar, if necessary, to make mixture a good spreading consistency. Stir in vanilla.

Yield: 2 cups.

Peanut Butter Frosting

Try the peanut butter frosting on chocolate cupcakes. Using butter instead of margarine and a good brand of peanut butter with this recipe results in a to-die-for frosting.

1 cup creamy peanut butter

1/2 cup butter, softened

2 cups confectioners' sugar

3 tablespoons milk or cream

In a large bowl, beat peanut butter and butter until light and fluffy with electric mixer. Slowly beat in the confectioner's sugar. Mix in milk or cream. Beat until frosting reaches a good spreading consistency, adding a little more cream or milk if necessary.

Yield: about 1 1/2 cups.

Whipped Cream Frosting

Create a frosting that is light yet delicious with just four ingredients.

1 1/2 cups whipping cream

3 tablespoons unsweetened cocoa powder

2 tablespoons confectioners' sugar

1 teaspoon vanilla extract

Combine all ingredients in a medium size bowl; beat until firm peaks form.

Yield: 3 cups.

Cream Cheese Frosting

Nothing is better than creamy cream cheese frosting on a carrot, chocolate or pumpkin cupcake.

1/2 cup butter or margarine, softened

1 (8 oz.) package cream cheese, softened

1 (16 oz.) package confectioners' sugar

1 teaspoon vanilla extract

In a medium bowl, mix together butter or margarine and cream cheese; beat until smooth. Add sugar and vanilla; beat until fluffy and light.

Yield: 3 cups.

Pineapple-Cream Cheese Frosting

This frosting is so delicious with the taste of pineapple mixed with cream cheese.

1 (8 oz.) can crushed pineapple

1 (8 oz.) package cream cheese, softened

1/4 cup butter or margarine, softened

1 (16 oz.) package confectioners' sugar

Drain pineapple and put into a sieve or strainer. Push pineapple against the sieve to force out additional juice; set aside. With an electric mixer at medium speed, beat cream cheese and butter until fluffy; gradually stir in confectioners' sugar and pineapple. (Frosting will be soft and may be refrigerated 1 hour before spreading over cake.)

Yield: 3 cups.

Peanut Butter Glaze

1 cup peanut butter

1/2 cup margarine

2 cups confectioners' sugar

3 tablespoons of milk

Beat the peanut butter and margarine together with mixer. Add the sugar and milk and mix well. Add more milk if needed for spreading.

Yield: about 1 1/2 cups.

Lemon-Flavored Frosting

Of course, this frosting is perfect for lemon cupcakes. Whipping cream can be substituted for heavy cream.

1 1/3 cups heavy cream

1/2 cup confectioners' sugar

1 tablespoon fresh lemon juice

With an electric mixer set on low, beat the cream in a chilled bowl until it begins to thicken. Add the confectioners' sugar and lemon juice, a little at a time, beating after each addition. With the mixer on high, beat about 5 minutes or until the frosting forms soft peaks.

Yield: about 3 cups.

Caramel Frosting

This frosting is exceptionally good on chocolate cupcakes.

3/4 cup packed brown sugar

1/3 cup half-and-half cream

1/4 cup butter, melted

1/2 teaspoon vanilla extract

1 3/4 cups confectioners' sugar

In a medium saucepan, combine the brown sugar, cream and butter. Bring to a boil, stirring frequently. Remove from the heat and stir in vanilla and confectioners' sugar. Beat with an electric mixer until fluffy, about 5 minutes.

Yield: about 1 1/2 cups.

Nutty Cream Cheese Frosting

This upgraded version of cream cheese frosting is a great compliment to white or yellow cupcakes.

1 (8-oz.) package cream cheese, softened

1/4 cup butter, softened

1 (16-oz.) package confectioners' sugar

1 teaspoon vanilla extract

1 cup chopped, toasted pecans

2 to 3 teaspoons milk

With an electric mixer at medium speed, beat cream cheese and butter until creamy. Slowly add confectioners' sugar, beating until fluffy and light. Add vanilla and pecans. Stir in 2 teaspoons milk, adding another teaspoon of milk, if necessary, for desired consistency.

Yield: 3 cups.

Peppermint Frosting

Peppermint oil has an intense, highly concentrated flavor like that found in chocolate covered peppermint patties.

1/2 cup margarine or butter, softened

1 (16-oz.) package confectioners' sugar

1/3 cup milk

1/4 teaspoon peppermint oil

With an electric mixer at medium speed, beat margarine or butter until creamy; slowly add confectioners' sugar alternately with milk. Beat at low speed just until blended after each addition. Stir in peppermint oil.

Yield: about 3 cups.

Toasted Pecan Frosting

Your cupcakes will quickly become a family favorite when you frost them with this delicious frosting.

1 cup chopped pecans

1 cup firmly packed light brown sugar

6 tablespoons whipping cream

6 tablespoons butter

1 teaspoon vanilla

1 cup confectioners' sugar

On a baking sheet, toast pecans at 350 degrees F for 15 minutes or until pecans are golden brown, stirring a few times. In a small saucepan over medium heat, bring brown sugar, cream and butter to a boil stirring often; boil for one minute, stirring constantly. Remove from heat; using a whisk, mix in vanilla and confectioners' sugar until smooth. Add toasted pecans; stir gently for three minutes or until frosting begins to cool and slightly thicken.

Yield: 1 1/2 cups.

Filling For Cupcakes

Biting into a yummy filling-in-the-center cupcake is definitely a sweet surprise.

1/2 cup sugar

1/3 cup vegetable oil

1/4 teaspoon salt

1 tablespoon water

1 teaspoon vanilla

1/3 cup milk

1/2 cup confectioners' sugar

With an electric mixer, beat the first five ingredients together very well. Add milk and beat again. Add confectioners' sugar and beat until mixed well. Use cake decorator to fill cupcakes using large round tip. Put into cupcakes and push.

Yield: 1 cup.

MUFFINS

Muffin Tips:

Using cupcake papers is a great way to keep a muffin pan clean. Spraying the cupcake papers with non-stick cooking spray will keep the muffins from sticking to the paper. Spraying the paper liners is a good idea especially if the muffin recipe is low-fat – otherwise you might be chewing the muffins off of the cupcake paper. Muffins are dryer than cupcakes.

Of course, paper liners are optional and just greasing the muffin pan will work also.

When mixing the muffin batter, after adding the liquid ingredients to the dry, stir just until the dry ingredients are moistened. The batter will still be lumpy. Over-mixed muffins may have a tough texture and become smooth on top.

Check for doneness with muffins by inserting a toothpick in the center of one, and if it comes out clean, the muffins are done. They also should be golden in color on top.

Remove the muffins from the pan immediately when they are done to keep muffin bottoms and sides from becoming soggy.

Apple Muffins

Applesauce Muffins

With ingredients like cloves, cinnamon and applesauce, these muffins are a great addition to a Christmas brunch or winter breakfast.

1 cup butter or margarine, softened
2 cups sugar
2 eggs
1 (16 oz.) can applesauce
1 teaspoon vanilla
2 teaspoons baking soda
4 cups all-purpose flour
1 1/2 teaspoons ground cinnamon
1 teaspoon ground allspice
1/2 teaspoon ground cloves

Using an electric mixer, cream butter or margarine at medium speed. Gradually add sugar, then eggs, beating well after each addition. In another bowl, combine applesauce, vanilla and baking soda. Mix together flour, cinnamon, allspice and cloves; add to butter mixture alternately with applesauce mixture, mixing after each addition.

Grease muffin cups or line with paper cupcake liners and fill two-thirds full of batter. Bake in preheated oven at 400 degrees F for 17 to 19 minutes or until inserted toothpick comes out clean. Yield: 30 muffins.

Apple Streusel Muffins

Chopped apples, combined with butter and cinnamon, create a chewy delicious muffin.

2 large eggs
1 cup sour cream
1/4 cup butter, melted
2 cups flour
1 cup sugar
1 tablespoon baking powder
1 1/4 teaspoons cinnamon
1/2 teaspoon salt
1 teaspoon vanilla
1/2 teaspoon baking soda
1 cup diced or chopped apples

STREUSEL TOPPING
1/4 cup sugar
3 tablespoons flour
1/4 teaspoon cinnamon
2 tablespoons butter

In a large bowl, beat eggs, sour cream, and butter. Add flour, sugar, baking powder, cinnamon, salt, vanilla and baking soda, along with apples and stir just until moistened. Grease muffin cups or line with paper cupcake liners and fill two-thirds full of batter.

Mix all streusel topping ingredients together. Sprinkle on topping. Bake in preheated oven at 400 degrees F for 20 to 25 minutes.

Yield: 18 muffins.

Banana Muffins

Chocolate Chip-Banana Muffins

Banana and chocolate are two great tastes that go well together. These muffins are quick and easy to make.

1 cup brown sugar
1/2 cup butter
3 bananas, mashed
2 eggs
2 cups flour
1/2 teaspoon baking powder
3/4 teaspoon baking soda
3/4 cup mini chocolate chips

Cream together brown sugar and butter. Add bananas and eggs to butter mixture and mix. Add flour, baking powder and baking soda; fold in chocolate chips and stir just until the dry ingredients are moistened. Grease muffin cups or line with paper cupcake liners and fill two-thirds full of batter. Bake in preheated oven at 350 degrees for 35 to 45 minutes.

Yield: 12 muffins.

Banana Muffins

These classic banana muffins are a great way to use overripe bananas while adding a kick of fiber to your day.

1 cup all-purpose flour
3 tablespoons sugar
2 1/2 teaspoons baking powder
1/2 teaspoon salt
1 cup whole bran
1 cup mashed ripe banana
1 beaten egg
1/4 cup milk
2 tablespoons vegetable oil or melted margarine

In a large bowl, combine flour, sugar, baking powder, and salt. Mix in bran. In another bowl, mix together banana, egg, milk, and oil or melted margarine. Add banana mixture to flour mixture, stirring just until dry ingredients are moistened. Grease muffin cups or line with paper cupcake liners and fill two-thirds full of batter. Bake muffins in preheated oven at 400 degrees F for 20 to 25 minutes or until inserted toothpick comes out clean.

Yield: 12 muffins.

Berry Muffins

Blueberry-Lemon Muffins

These muffins have a delicious combination of lemon juice, blueberries and cinnamon.

3/4 cup sugar
3 tablespoons vegetable oil
1 egg
3/4 cup milk
1 tablespoon lemon juice
1 teaspoon baking soda
1 teaspoon cinnamon
1 teaspoon salt
1 1/2 cups flour (1/2 whole wheat and 1/2 white)
1 cup frozen or fresh blueberries

Mix sugar, oil, egg, milk, and lemon juice together by hand or with mixer on low. Add baking soda, cinnamon, salt and flour. Fold in blueberries. Grease muffin cups or line with paper cupcake liners and fill two-thirds full of batter. Bake in preheated oven at 400 degrees F for 20 to 25 minutes.

Yield: 12 muffins.

The Best Blueberry Muffins

The blueberries and sweet batter are great together in these easy-to-make muffins.

1/2 cup butter or margarine
1 cup sugar
2 large eggs
2 teaspoons baking powder
1 teaspoon vanilla
1/4 teaspoon salt
2 cups flour
1/2 cup milk
2 1/2 cups frozen or fresh blueberries

Topping:
1/4 teaspoon ground nutmeg
1 tablespoon sugar

Beat butter and sugar until fluffy and light. Add eggs, one at a time, beating after each addition. Beat in baking powder, vanilla and salt. Fold 1/2 of the flour, then 1/2 of the milk into the batter. Repeat with the remaining flour and milk. Stir just until the dry ingredients are moistened. Carefully fold in blueberries.

Grease muffin cups or line with paper cupcake liners and fill two-thirds full of batter. Sprinkle with combined topping ingredients. Bake in preheated oven at 375 degrees F for 30 minutes, until tops are golden and top feels springy to the touch when pressed.

Yield: 18 muffins.

Raspberry Sour Cream Muffins

Sour cream is the secret ingredient in these raspberry muffins, resulting in a moist, rich muffin.

1 cup flour
1 teaspoon baking powder
1/2 teaspoon baking soda
1/2 teaspoon salt
2 eggs
1 cup sour cream
5 tablespoons butter
1 cup brown sugar
1 cup old-fashioned oatmeal
1 cup fresh or frozen raspberries

Combine flour, baking powder, baking soda and salt. In a separate bowl, mix together the eggs and sour cream. In a saucepan, melt together the butter and brown sugar. Add the brown sugar mixture to the egg mixture, then add the oats. Fold in flour mixture. Stir just until the dry ingredients are moistened. Carefully fold in raspberries.

Grease muffin cups or line with paper cupcake liners and fill two-thirds full of batter. Drop a pinch of sugar on top of each. Bake in preheated oven at 375 degrees for 25 minutes.

Yield: 24 muffins.

Cranberry Pumpkin Muffins

The tart cranberries combined with spicy cloves and cinnamon are a perfect complement to the pumpkin in these muffins. Dried cherries can be substituted for cranberries.

1 1/2 cups flour
1 teaspoon baking soda
1/4 teaspoon baking powder
1/2 teaspoon cinnamon
1/2 teaspoon ground cloves
1/4 teaspoon salt
1 1/4 cups sugar
1/4 cup butter, softened
2 eggs
1 cup canned pumpkin
1 cup cranberries, coarsely chopped
1/2 cup walnuts, chopped

In a bowl, combine flour, baking soda, baking powder, cinnamon, cloves and salt. In a large bowl, cream together sugar and butter until fluffy and light. Add eggs one at a time. Add pumpkin. Add flour mixture; stir just until moistened. Fold cranberries into batter.

Grease muffin cups or line with paper cupcake liners and fill with batter to top of cup. Sprinkle muffins with walnuts. Bake in preheated oven at 400 degrees F for 20 to 25 minutes.

Yield: 18 muffins.

Cherry Muffins

If you love cherries, this may become your favorite recipe.

2 cups flour
3/4 cup sugar
2 teaspoons baking powder
1/4 teaspoon salt
2 eggs, slightly beaten
3/4 cup milk
2 tablespoons margarine, melted
2 cups pitted fresh tart cherries or 1 can (16 oz.) pie cherries, drained

Mix 1 1/2 cups of the flour, sugar, baking powder and salt in a medium bowl. Mix eggs, milk and margarine in a small bowl. Stir egg mixture into dry ingredients just until moistened.

Mix cherries with remaining 1/2 cup flour in a small bowl; fold into batter. Grease muffin cups or line with paper cupcake liners and fill two-thirds full of batter. Bake in preheated oven at 400 degrees F until golden, about 20 minutes.

Yield: 12 muffins.

Bran Muffins

Moist Bran Muffins

This batter can be made ahead, stored in the refrigerator and baked as needed.

5 cups all-purpose flour
3 cups sugar
1 quart buttermilk
1 cup vegetable oil
4 large eggs
1 tablespoon plus 2 teaspoons baking soda
1 tablespoon plus 1 teaspoon ground cinnamon
2 teaspoons salt
1 (17 oz.) can fruit cocktail, do not drain
1 (15 oz.) package wheat bran flakes cereal with raisins

Combine all ingredients in a large mixing bowl; beat at medium speed with an electric mixer 2 minutes. Grease muffin cups or line with paper cupcake liners and fill two-thirds full of batter. Bake in preheated oven at 400 degrees F for 16 to 18 minutes or until inserted toothpick comes out clean.

Yield: 4 1/2 dozen.

Oatmeal Bran Muffins

These sweet oatmeal and bran muffins will make a nice, hearty snack.

2 cups boiling water
2 cups 100% bran buds cereal
1 cup sugar
1 cup brown sugar
1 cup vegetable oil
4 eggs
5 cups flour
1 quart buttermilk
1 teaspoon salt
5 teaspoons baking soda
4 cups uncooked oatmeal
1 cup chopped nuts, raisins or dates

Pour boiling water over bran and set aside. Cream sugar, brown sugar and oil. Add eggs, flour, buttermilk, salt and baking soda; mix well. Add oatmeal and bran and stir just until well moistened. Fold in nuts, raisins or dates. Grease muffin cups or line with paper cupcake liners and fill two-thirds full of batter. Bake in preheated oven at 375 degrees F for 15 to 20 minutes.

Yield: 8 dozen muffins.

No-Sugar Banana-Bran Muffins

Keep calories low without losing flavor with these easy-to-make banana bran muffins.

8 large overripe bananas, mashed
3 cups all-bran extra fiber cereal
2 cups skim milk
2 eggs
1/4 cup olive oil
1 cup raisins
3 cups self-rising flour
1 cup chopped pecans

Combine bananas, fiber cereal, milk, eggs, oil and raisins in a large bowl. Add flour, 1 cup at a time, mixing after each addition. Add pecans. Grease muffin cups or line with paper cupcake liners and lightly spray paper liners with non-stick cooking spray. Fill two-thirds full of batter. Bake in preheated oven at 425 degrees F for 25 minutes.

Yield: 30 muffins.

*Note: If self-rising flour is not available, it's easy to make. For 3 cups of self-rising flour, use 3 cups of all-purpose flour, 4 1/2 teaspoons baking powder and 3/4 teaspoon salt. Whisk to combine.

Chocolate Muffins

Fudge Brownie Muffins

Decadent brownie indulgence in the form of a muffin.

1/2 cup butter or margarine
1/4 cup unsweetened cocoa powder
1 cup sugar
2 large eggs, lightly beaten
1 teaspoon vanilla
3/4 cup all-purpose flour
1 teaspoon ground cinnamon
1/4 cup chopped pecans
Semisweet chocolate chips

Mix butter or margarine and cocoa together in a microwavable bowl; microwave on HIGH for 1 minute or until butter melts. Set aside. In a medium bowl, combine sugar, eggs and vanilla Add butter mixture, flour, cinnamon and nuts. Stir just until the dry ingredients are moistened.

Grease muffin cups or line with paper cupcake liners and fill two-thirds full of batter. Sprinkle each muffin with 6 to 8 chocolate chips. Bake in preheated oven at 350 degrees F for 20 minutes or until an inserted toothpick comes out clean.

Yield: 10 muffins.

Chocolate Toffee Muffins

Rich chocolate muffins! Tasty, moist and full of chocolate goodness.

1 1/4 cups milk
1 egg
1/3 cup vegetable oil
2 cups flour
2/3 cup sugar
1/3 cup unsweetened cocoa powder
2 teaspoons baking powder
1/2 teaspoon salt
3 bars chocolate-covered English toffee candy (1.4 oz. each)

In a large bowl, combine milk, egg and oil; beat well by hand. Add flour, sugar, cocoa, baking powder and salt; mix just until dry ingredients are moistened. Chop each candy bar into small pieces. Set aside 1/4 cup of toffee candy; mix remaining candy pieces into batter.

Grease bottoms only of muffin cups or line with paper baking cups. Divide batter evenly among muffin cups. Sprinkle each muffin with the reserved candy. Bake in preheated oven at 400 degrees F for 18 to 20 minutes, or until inserted toothpick comes out clean.

Yield: 12 muffins.

Chocolate Pecan Muffins

This is a simple recipe that is not too sweet. These muffins are even better the next day.

3/4 cup chopped pecans
1 cup all-purpose flour
3/4 cup whole wheat flour
1/2 cup sugar
1/3 cup unsweetened cocoa powder
2 teaspoons baking powder
2 teaspoons espresso powder
1/2 teaspoon salt
2 eggs
1 cup milk
1 teaspoon vanilla
1/2 cup melted butter

Toast pecans in a 350 degree F oven until color darkens slightly. Remove and let cool.

In a bowl, blend together flour, wheat flour, sugar, cocoa, baking powder, espresso powder and salt. In a separate bowl, whisk eggs, vanilla, butter and milk until blended. Add liquid ingredients to the dry and stir until mixed well. Stir in pecans.

Butter muffin cups or line with paper cupcake liners and divide batter evenly into 12 muffin cups. Bake in preheated oven at 400 degrees F for 15 to 20 minutes until tops are lightly browned and toothpick comes out clean.

Yield: 12 muffins.

Nut Muffins

Macadamia Nut Muffins

Macadamia nuts and chocolate chips make for an irresistible muffin.

2 cups unbleached flour
1/2 cup sugar
1 teaspoon baking powder
1/2 teaspoon baking soda
1/2 teaspoon salt
3/4 cup dairy sour cream
1/2 cup margarine or butter, melted
1/4 cup milk
1 tablespoon vanilla
1 egg
1/2 cup chopped macadamia nuts
1/2 cup miniature semi-sweet chocolate chips

Streusel
1/4 cup flour
1/4 cup brown sugar, firmly packed
2 tablespoons margarine or butter

In a small bowl, combine all streusel ingredients; blend with fork until mixture resembles coarse crumbs. Set aside.

In large bowl, combine flour, sugar, baking powder, baking soda and salt; mix well. Add sour cream, 1/2 cup margarine or butter, milk, vanilla and egg to flour mixture; stir just until moistened. Fold in macadamia nuts and chocolate chips.

Grease muffin cups or line with paper cupcake liners and fill 3/4 full of batter. Sprinkle each with 1 1/2 teaspoons of streusel. Bake in preheated oven at 375 degrees F for 18 to 20 minutes or until inserted toothpick comes out clean.

Yield: 18 muffins.

Date Nut Muffins

These date and nut muffins are easy and delicious. Decorate with buttercream frosting, grated chocolate and candied cherries.

1 (8 oz.) package pitted dates, coarsely chopped
3/4 cup boiling water
1/4 cup corn oil
1/2 teaspoon vanilla
1 cup flour
1/2 cup whole wheat flour
1/2 cup sugar
1/3 cup chopped walnuts
1/2 teaspoon baking soda

In a large bowl, combine all ingredients. Stir well. Grease muffin cups or line with paper cupcake liners and fill two-thirds full of batter. Bake in preheated oven at 375 degrees F for 25 minutes.

Yield: 12 muffins.

Orange Muffins

Mandarin Orange Muffins

These muffins with an orange twist are perfect for a snack or light breakfast.

2 cups flour
2/3 cup sugar
1 teaspoon baking powder
1/4 teaspoon salt
1/2 teaspoon baking soda
1/3 cup vegetable oil
2 teaspoons grated orange rind
1 (11 oz.) can mandarin oranges, drained and halved
1/2 cup orange juice
1/2 cup plain yogurt
1 egg, beaten

Mix flour, sugar, baking powder, salt and baking soda; cut in vegetable oil until coarse crumbs form. Stir in orange rind and halved orange segments. In a small bowl, mix together orange juice, yogurt and egg until blended. Add to dry ingredients; stir just until moistened.

Grease muffin cups or line with paper cupcake liners and fill two-thirds full of batter. Bake in preheated oven at 400 degrees F for 20 minutes or until inserted toothpick comes out clean.

Yield: 16 muffins.

Strawberry-Orange Muffins

The strawberry-orange touch adds a special taste to ordinary muffins.

2 1/4 cups all-purpose flour
2 teaspoons baking powder
1 teaspoon baking soda
1/2 teaspoon salt
3/4 cup sugar
1 egg
1/2 cup sour cream
1/2 cup milk
1/3 cup vegetable oil
1 tablespoon orange peel, finely grated
1 cup fresh or frozen thawed strawberries
1/3 cup strawberry jam

Slice strawberries very thin, about 1/8 inch thick. Pat strawberries dry between paper towels to keep their juices from coloring the batter. In a large bowl, mix together flour, baking powder, baking soda and salt; set aside. In a medium bowl, whisk together sugar, egg, sour cream, milk, oil and orange peel until mixed; fold in the strawberries. Add the wet ingredients to the dry ingredients and stir just until moistened.

Grease muffin cups or line with paper cupcake liners. Put a large spoonful of batter in each muffin cup. Add one teaspoon of strawberry jam on top of the batter in each cup. Add the rest of the batter on top of the jam, filling each muffin cup about two-thirds full. Bake in preheated oven at 400 degrees F for 15 to 18 minutes, or until an inserted toothpick comes out clean. Yield: 16 muffins.

Orange Blossom Muffins

Savor the taste of orange, cinnamon and pecans for breakfast.

2 cups Bisquick
1/4 cup sugar
1 egg, slightly beaten
1/2 cup orange juice
2 tablespoons vegetable oil
1/2 cup chopped pecans
1/2 cup orange marmalade
3 tablespoons sugar
1 tablespoon all-purpose flour
1/2 teaspoon ground cinnamon
1/4 teaspoon ground nutmeg

Combine Bisquick and 1/4 cup sugar in a large bowl. Combine egg, orange juice and oil; add to biscuit mixture, stirring just until moistened. Stir in pecans and marmalade.

Grease muffin cups or line with paper cupcake liners and fill two-thirds full of batter. Combine 3 tablespoons sugar, flour, cinnamon and nutmeg; sprinkle evenly over batter. Bake in preheated oven at 400 degrees F for 18 minutes or until inserted toothpick comes out clean.

Yield: 12 muffins.

Miscellaneous Muffins

Oatmeal Muffins

You can probably find most of the ingredients for these simple muffins in your kitchen pantry.

1 cup oatmeal
1 cup buttermilk
1 egg, beaten well
1/2 cup brown sugar
1/2 cup vegetable oil
1 cup flour
1 teaspoon baking soda
1/4 teaspoon salt

Soak oatmeal in buttermilk for 10 to 15 minutes. (Can substitute for buttermilk: 1 cup milk with 1 teaspoon lemon juice.) Add egg. Add brown sugar, oil, flour, baking soda and salt; mix well. Grease muffin cups or line with paper cupcake liners and fill two-thirds full of batter. Bake in preheated oven for 15 minutes at 400 degrees.

Yield: 12 muffins.

Zucchini Date Muffins

This muffin recipe proves that eating healthy can also be mouthwatering good.

3/4 cup rolled oats
1 cup whole wheat flour
1 1/2 teaspoons cinnamon
1 teaspoon baking powder
1 teaspoon baking soda
1 cup grated zucchini
1/2 cup chopped dates
1 teaspoon orange zest, grated
1/2 cup sunflower seeds or chopped nuts
1/4 cup honey or molasses
1/2 cup yogurt
1/4 cup vegetable oil
1 egg

Mix together oats, flour, cinnamon, baking powder, baking soda, zucchini, dates, orange zest and chopped nuts or sunflower seeds. In a separate bowl, combine honey or molasses, yogurt, oil and egg. Add dry mixture to the liquid mixture, stirring just until moistened.

Grease muffin cups or line with paper cupcake liners and fill two-thirds full of batter. Bake in preheated oven at 375 degrees F for 20 to 25 minutes.

Yield: 12 muffins.

Cinnamon Puffs

These cinnamon puffs are easy and inexpensive to make.

1/3 cup butter or margarine, melted
1/2 cup sugar
1 egg
1 1/2 cups all-purpose flour
1 1/2 teaspoons baking powder
1/2 teaspoon salt
1/4 teaspoon ground cinnamon
1/2 cup milk

In a large bowl, mix by hand butter, sugar and egg. Mix flour, baking powder, salt and cinnamon; stir into egg mixture alternately with milk, mixing just until dry ingredients are moistened.

Grease muffin cups or line with paper cupcake liners and fill two-thirds full of batter. Bake in preheated oven at 350 degrees F for 20 to 25 minutes or until golden brown.

Dipping Mixture
1/2 cup sugar
1 teaspoon ground cinnamon
1/2 cup butter or margarine, melted

Mix sugar and cinnamon. Immediately after removing from oven, dip tops of puffs in butter, then in cinnamon-sugar mixture. Serve warm.

Yield: 12 puffs.

Key Lime Muffins

The fresh lime flavor of these muffins makes them the perfect choice to serve with a cup of tea.

2 cups all-purpose flour
1 cup sugar
1 tablespoon baking powder
1/2 teaspoon salt
2 large eggs, lightly beaten
1/3 cup milk
1/4 cup vegetable oil
1/4 cup key lime juice
1 teaspoon grated lime rind

In a large bowl, mix together flour, sugar, baking powder and salt. Combine eggs, milk, oil, lime juice and lime rind; add to flour mixture, stirring just until moistened. Grease muffin cups or line with paper cupcake liners and fill three-quarters full of batter. Bake muffins in preheated oven at 400 degrees for 18 minutes or until light brown on top.

Yield: 12 muffins.

Hawaiian Pineapple Muffins

A delicious muffin that's sweetened with pineapple. Hearty and satisfying!

2 cups Bisquick
1/4 cup sugar
2 tablespoons butter or margarine
1 egg
2/3 cup milk
1/2 cup drained crushed pineapple
Thin icing (recipe below)

Mix Bisquick, sugar, butter or margarine, egg, and milk with fork. Beat for 30 seconds. Fold in pineapple. Grease muffin cups or line with paper cupcake liners and fill two-thirds full of batter. Bake in preheated oven for 15 to 20 minutes in 375 degrees F oven. Frost while warm.

Thin Icing:
Blend 1/2 cup confectioner's sugar and 1 tablespoon water until smooth. Sprinkle with 1 cup chopped nuts.

Yield: 12 muffins.

Best-Ever Muffins

Plain or with the suggested sweet additions, these versatile muffins are sure to be a hit.

1 3/4 cups all-purpose flour
2 tablespoons sugar
2 1/2 teaspoons baking powder
3/4 teaspoon salt
1 egg, beaten well
3/4 cup milk
1/3 cup vegetable oil or melted margarine

Combine flour, sugar, baking powder and salt; make well in center. Combine egg, milk, and vegetable oil or margarine. Add egg mixture to dry mixture. Mix only until dry ingredients are moistened. Grease muffin cups or line with paper cupcake liners and fill two-thirds full of batter. Bake in preheated oven at 400 degrees F for 25 minutes.

Yield: 12 muffins.

Easy ways to dress up Best-Ever Muffins:

Blueberry Muffins: Prepare batter, using only 1/2 cup milk. Combine 2 tablespoons of sugar and 1 cup fresh or well-drained frozen blueberries. Stir gently into batter.

Raisin, Nut, or Date Muffins: Add 1/2 to 3/4 cup seedless raisins, broken nuts, or coarsely cut dates to batter.

Cranberry Muffins: Prepare batter; fill muffin pans 1/3 full. Cut 1 cup canned jellied cranberry sauce into 1/2 inch cubes; sprinkle over batter. Spoon remaining batter on top.

Jelly Muffins: Top batter in each muffin pan with 1 teaspoon tart jelly before baking.

Sour-milk Muffins: Substitute 3/4 cup sour milk or buttermilk for sweet milk. Add 1/4 teaspoon soda and reduce baking powder to 1 teaspoon and reduce baking powder to 1 teaspoon. Mix soda with dry ingredients.

Sugar-crusted Muffins: Bake Best-ever Muffins. While hot, dip tops in 1/2 cup melted butter; shake in a mixture of 1/2 cup sugar and 1 teaspoon cinnamon. Serve warm.

Rainbow Muffins

Moist and colorful, these muffins are perfect for a child's birthday party or summertime picnic.

2 1/4 cups Bisquick
1/4 cup sugar
1/4 teaspoon ginger
1 egg
2/3 cup milk
3/4 cup canned fruit cocktail, drained

Ginger Sugar:
1 tablespoon sugar
1/4 teaspoon ginger

In a large bowl, blend Bisquick, sugar and ginger. In a medium bowl, beat egg slightly; add milk to egg. Add egg mixture to dry mixture, blending just until moistened, then add fruit cocktail, mixing in gently. Grease muffin cups or line with paper cupcake liners and fill two-thirds full of batter. Mix ginger sugar ingredients together and sprinkle on top of batter.

Bake in preheated oven at 400 degrees F for 18 to 20 minutes or until done.

Yield: 9 muffins.

Coffeecake Muffins

Delicate little muffins layered with crunchy-sweet, zesty nuts. They're company-good served with a cup of fresh-brewed coffee.

1 1/2 cups all-purpose flour
1/2 cup sugar
2 teaspoons baking powder
1/2 teaspoon salt
1/4 cup shortening
1/2 cup milk
1 egg, beaten

Mix together flour, sugar, baking powder and salt; cut in shortening until dough is similar to coarse crumbs. Combine milk and egg; add to flour mixture; stir just until the dry ingredients are moistened. Alternate layers of batter and Zesty Nuts (recipe below) in greased or paper lined muffin pans, (ending with batter), filling two-thirds full. Bake in preheated oven at 375 degrees F for about 20 minutes. Top with zesty nuts.

Yield: 12 muffins.

Zesty Nuts:
1/2 cup brown sugar
1/2 cup walnuts or pecans, chopped
2 tablespoons flour
2 teaspoons cinnamon
2 tablespoons melted butter

Combine all zesty nuts ingredients.

Peanut Butter Muffins

Enjoy a cold glass of milk and a delicious peanut butter muffin for a treat that can't be beat.

2 cups all-purpose flour
1/2 cup sugar
2 1/2 teaspoons baking powder
1/2 teaspoon salt
2 tablespoons butter
1/2 cup crunchy peanut butter
3/4 cup milk
2 eggs, well beaten
1/4 cup currant jelly or grape jelly, melted
1/2 cup peanuts, finely chopped

Mix together flour, sugar, baking powder and salt. Cut in butter and peanut butter until mixture is similar to coarse crumbs. Stir in eggs and milk all at once, mixing just until moistened.

Grease muffin cups or line with paper cupcake liners and fill two-thirds full of batter. Bake in preheated oven at 400 degrees F for 15 to 17 minutes. Remove from oven and brush tops with melted jelly; dip in peanuts. Serve hot.

Yield: 22 muffins.

Peaches 'N Cream

Tasty bran muffins with sweet peaches and cream to enjoy right out of the oven.

1 (4 oz.) package cream cheese
1 (14 oz.) can sliced peaches, drained
2 eggs
1 1/4 cups milk
1/3 cup honey
1/4 cup butter, melted
1 teaspoon grated lemon rind
1 1/2 cups bran cereal
2 cups all-purpose flour
1 tablespoon baking powder
1 teaspoon cinnamon
1/2 teaspoon salt

Chop cream cheese and peaches into cubes; set aside. Beat eggs lightly with fork in a large bowl. To egg, add milk, honey, butter and lemon rind; mix well. Add cereal. Combine flour, baking powder, cinnamon and salt in large bowl; mix well. Add cream cheese and peaches to the cereal mixture. Add cereal mixture to flour mixture, mixing just until moist.

Grease muffin cups or line with paper cupcake liners and fill to the top with batter. Bake in preheated oven at 400 degrees F for 20 to 25 minutes or until inserted toothpick comes out clean.

Yield: 24 muffins.

Morning Glory Muffins

What a wonderful way to start a day with the healthy flavors of carrots, apples, coconut, raisins and walnuts in a take-along muffin.

2 cups flour
1 1/4 cups sugar
2 teaspoons cinnamon
2 teaspoons baking soda
1/2 teaspoon salt
1 1/2 cups grated apples
1 1/2 cups shredded carrots
3/4 cup coconut
1/2 cup walnuts, chopped
1/2 cup dried cranberries or raisins
1/2 cup applesauce
1/2 cup vegetable oil
3 eggs, beaten
1 teaspoon vanilla

Combine flour, sugar, cinnamon, baking soda and salt. In a separate bowl, mix together apples, carrots, coconut, walnuts and cranberries or raisins. Stir in applesauce, oil, eggs and vanilla, and add to dry ingredients. Stir until moistened. Grease muffin cups or line with paper cupcake liners and fill to top with batter. Bake in preheated oven at 375 degrees F for 18 to 20 minutes.

Yield: 24 muffins.

Peach and Brown Sugar Muffins

Make muffins that taste like a scrumptious peach cobbler with this recipe.

4 cups flour
2/3 cup packed brown sugar
2 teaspoons baking powder
1/2 teaspoon allspice
1/2 teaspoon baking soda
1 teaspoon salt
2 cups sour cream
1/2 cup vegetable oil
2 eggs
1 cup fresh, frozen or canned peaches, chopped

In a large bowl, combine flour, brown sugar, baking powder, allspice, baking soda and salt. In another bowl, combine sour cream, oil and eggs; mix well and fold in peaches. Add peach mixture to the flour mixture; stirring just until moistened. Batter will be lumpy. Line muffin cups with paper cupcake liners or lightly grease and fill two-thirds full of batter. Bake in preheated oven at 400 degrees F 20 to 25 minutes or until tops are golden.

Yield: 20 muffins.

Cupcake Cones

Kids love these fun-to-make and fun-to-eat cupcake cones. This recipe is for yellow cake. If you prefer white cake, use the Simple White Cupcakes recipe.

2/3 cup margarine, softened
2 eggs
1 3/4 cups sugar
1 1/2 teaspoons vanilla
2 3/4 cups flour
2 1/2 teaspoons baking powder
1 teaspoon salt
1 1/4 cups milk
24 flat-bottom ice cream cones, 2" to 3" high
One of the frosting recipes in this book or 2 cans prepared frosting
Plain or peanut chocolate candies
Candy sprinkles, toasted coconut or nuts, as desired

In a large bowl, cream margarine, eggs, sugar and vanilla with electric mixer until light and fluffy. In another bowl, combine flour, baking powder and salt; add alternately with milk to wet ingredients. Beat to a soft smooth batter.

Fill each cone with 3 tablespoons batter. Place on ungreased cookie sheet about 3 inches apart or place cones in muffin tins. Bake in preheated oven at 350 degrees F for 30 to 35 minutes or until inserted toothpick comes out clean. Cool thoroughly. Frost; decorate with candies and toppings.

Yield: 24 cupcake cones.

Tarts and Mini Pies in Muffin Cups

Cream Cheese Cherry Tarts

You just can't beat the fabulous taste of cherry with cream cheese on a vanilla wafer crust.

2 (8 oz.) package cream cheese, softened
2 eggs
3/4 cup sugar
1 teaspoon vanilla
16 to 25 vanilla wafers
1 (21 oz.) can cherry pie filling

Beat cream cheese until smooth; beat in eggs. Add sugar and vanilla. Line muffin tins with paper cupcake liners. Place vanilla wafer in bottom of liner, then fill with cream cheese mixture, about half-full. Bake in preheated oven at 350 degrees F for 15 to 20 minutes. Cool and top with cherry pie filling. Refrigerate.

Yield: 16 to 24 tarts.

Coffee Nut Tortoni

This light and fluffy dessert doesn't go into an oven but instead firms up in the freezer. Elegant and very easy!

1 cup whipping cream or heavy cream
1/4 cup sugar
1 tablespoon instant coffee
1 teaspoon vanilla extract
1/2 teaspoon almond extract
1 egg white
2 tablespoons sugar
1/4 cup flaked coconut
1/4 cup almonds, finely chopped
8 - 10 maraschino cherries

With an electric mixer, whip cream on medium speed. Add 1/4 cup sugar, coffee, vanilla and almond extract. In another bowl, beat egg white until soft peaks form. While beating, gradually add 2 tablespoons sugar to egg white and beat to stiff peaks.

Combine coconut and almonds. Fold egg white and half the almond mixture into the cream. Spoon into 8 or 10 foil cupcake papers placed in muffin cups. Sprinkle remaining nut mixture over tops. Top each with a cherry. Freeze until firm.

Yield: 8 to 10 desserts.

Mint Chocolate Mini-Pies

Very rich and yummy for "just a bite of dessert".

2 cups confectioners' sugar
1 cup butter
4 (1 oz.) squares unsweetened chocolate, melted
4 eggs
1 teaspoon peppermint flavoring
2 teaspoons vanilla
18 vanilla wafers
1 cup heavy cream whipped
1/2 cup pecan pieces
18 maraschino cherries

Cream sugar and butter until fluffy and light. Add melted chocolate. Add eggs and beat well, then mix in peppermint flavoring and vanilla. Put a vanilla wafer in the bottom of paper cupcake liners. Fill with chocolate mixture 3/4 full. Add a dollop of whipped cream on top. Sprinkle with pecans and place a cherry on top. Freeze in muffin tins to keep shape. Serve frozen.

Yield: 18 mini-pies.

Miniature Cheesecakes

These mini desserts are so cute and keep the calories down by being just a small indulgence.

2 eggs
2 (8 oz.) pkg. cream cheese, softened
3/4 cup sugar
1 teaspoon vanilla
1 tablespoon lemon juice
24 vanilla wafers
1 can cherry pie filling (or desired filling)

In a medium bowl, beat eggs, cream cheese, sugar, vanilla and lemon juice until fluffy and light. Put a vanilla wafer in the bottom of paper cupcake liners. Fill liners three-quarters full of cream cheese mixture. Bake in preheated oven at 350 degrees F for 15 to 20 minutes or until set. Top each with a spoonful of pie filling. Keep refrigerated.

Yield: 24 mini cheesecakes.

Other Books by Victoria Steele

101 Quick & Easy Chicken Recipes

101 Quick & Easy Cookie Recipes

All titles available in Paperback and Kindle versions at Amazon.com

Photo credits:

Photos by

Robert Linton

LuminaStock

Graphics by

ElsyStudio

Portare Fortuna

Made in the USA
Lexington, KY
11 May 2018